BEING WITH GOD

A Bible and prayer guide
for people with dementia

WORDS OF
FAITH

Also in the **Being with God** series: *Words of hope, Words of peace.*

Copyright © Scripture Union 2010

ISBN: 9781844275212

Scripture Union, 207–209 Queensway, Bletchley,
Milton Keynes, MK2 2EB, England
Email: info@scriptureunion.org.uk
Website: www.scriptureunion.org.uk

Scripture Union USA, PO Box 987, Valley Forge, PA 19482, USA
Email: info@scriptureunion.org
Website: www.scriptureunion.org

Scripture Union Australia, Locked Bag 2, Central Coast Business Centre,
NSW 2252, Australia
Website: www.scriptureunion.org.au

Scripture quotations, unless otherwise indicated, are taken from the HOLY BIBLE,
NEW INTERNATIONAL VERSION. Copyright © 1973, 1978, 1984 by International
Bible Society. Anglicisation copyright © 1979, 1984, 1989, 1995, 1996, 2001.
Used by permission of Hodder & Stoughton Ltd.

British Library Cataloguing-in-Publication Data: a catalogue record of this book
is available from the British Library.

Developed and edited by 'Tricia Williams
Expert consultant and introduction: Margaret Goodall
All recordings produced by Gordon Lorenz

Cover design and internal layout by Martin Lore
Printed and bound in Singapore by Tien Wah Press Ltd

Scripture Union is an international Christian charity working with churches
in more than 130 countries providing resources to bring the good news of Jesus
Christ to children, young people and families and to encourage them to develop
spiritually through the Bible and prayer. As well as coordinating a network of
volunteers, staff and associates who run holidays, church-based events and school
Christian groups, Scripture Union produces a wide range of publications and
supports those who use their resources through training programmes.

> '**DRAW NIGH TO GOD,
> AND HE WILL
> DRAW NIGH TO YOU.**'
>
> *James 4:8, KJV*

FOR RON AND JUDY

CONTENTS

FOREWORD

Dementia is a cruel robber. It robs people of their memory, their personality, their ability to recognise and react normally even with partners and family they've loved for years. In short, it robs them of themselves and the life they've known. Confusion and strangeness replace the familiar and safe. They have a whole lifetime of experience and knowledge behind them – yet that knowledge is tantalisingly beyond their mind's grasp.

The knowledge which escapes them may well include a lifelong faith in God and a love of his word in the Bible which has been a constant source of strength and reassurance during challenging times in the past. However, with the onset of dementia, that comfort is lost to them as much-loved biblical stories, prayers and hymns are frustratingly hard to remember.

With its carefully chosen mix of familiar words and evocative music, this imaginative and practical resource is nothing less than a Godsend – a nudge to the memory which at its most obvious level is a delightful way to aid conversation and recall, but at its deepest, opens, for the person with dementia, a real connection to faith and the God who has never stopped loving them.

Pam Rhodes
Presenter of BBC's Songs of Praise,
Patron of Methodist Homes for the Aged

WELCOME
AND THANKS

We hope that you will find this Bible and prayer guide brings you God's blessing and comfort – whether you are the person with dementia or you are a 'carer'.

This resource has been developed specifically for people with dementia, but older people who are struggling with memory loss may also find it helpful.

We are so grateful for the help and encouragement of many in the creation of this resource. **Margaret Goodall**, Chaplaincy Advisor for **MHA**, has given constant encouragement as our expert consultant. We've also much appreciated help and advice from **Christian Council on Ageing** and **Alzheimer's Society**. Individuals facing the challenges of dementia have given invaluable feedback on the content. We are especially grateful for the support and encouragement of **Pam Rhodes**, presenter of BBC's **Songs of Praise**, Patron of MHA.

Our thanks too to all those who have given towards the development of these resources – including: MHA, Christian Council on Ageing and Social Interface Ltd – whose generosity has helped enormously in the creation of this resource.

Words of faith: the CD

With its familiar hymns and evocative performances, this CD has been specially produced and compiled for inclusion in this guide. It would not have been possible without the generous support of Gordon Lorenz, music producer, and of the professional and highly gifted performers he has brought together. Our thanks to all of those who been involved in these recordings, and for their great creativity and sensitivity in bringing us this music.

Our prayer is that – as you use this guide – you will know that God is close to you, as you draw near to him.

'Tricia Williams
Editor

INTRODUCTION

A WORD FOR CARERS

Some older people, either because they are living with dementia or because of age, are no longer able to join in public worship. The following pages offer a way to help them reconnect with the Christian faith and story.

People with dementia are sometimes thought of as no longer being able to worship. But even when people have not spoken for a while – as those involved in their care will know – they are still able to join in with familiar prayers and hymns. We need to offer clues as to what is going on, a context for worship, and cues in the words that are so familiar, in order to help them join in.

As the effects of dementia increase, it is more difficult to interact with others and to be understood. But while thoughts and words may be confused, feelings and emotions experienced are still real. So if we can meet people on an emotional or 'feeling' level instead of the rational or thinking level, then we meet people who are like us but who need help to be part of the world around them.

I hope that by using this Bible and prayer guide, people who could be isolated by dementia, will be helped to feel once again part of the Christian community, and be reminded that God loves and accepts them as they are – something we all need reminding of.

We believe in a God who can reach beyond our reasoning and understanding of words to touch us again with his love.

Margaret Goodall
Chaplaincy Advisor, MHA

HOW TO USE
THIS GUIDE

SETTING THE SCENE

In order to use this Bible and prayer guide to best effect it will be important to 'set the scene' so that the person with dementia can recognise what is going to happen. Imagine what it's like to wake up in a strange place. For a moment all is odd and 'wrong'. For those with dementia it is always like this. So, as carers, we need to do all we can to help them focus.

Using the same setting each time we use this guide can help provide a way of 'cueing in' and be a reminder of what is about to take place. For example, a small table, with a white cloth and a Bible, cross or prayer book could make any room into the place where we regularly take time to 'be with God'. If possible, use the same Bible each time.

The same words used to introduce the session could become a familiar part of this time and again provide a cue into worship. The words need to be simple and easy to remember, affirming God's presence. For example:

God is here
God is always here

God is with us
God is always with us

EACH DAY'S DEVOTIONAL

Each day's devotional follows a regular format which it is hoped, for some, may become a familiar prompt for this special time with God. We understand that each person with dementia (or elderly person struggling with memory loss) is an individual and will be at different stages in facing the challenges of dementia or age. For this reason, the devotionals aren't intended to be scripts. Feel free to take the suggestions here and use what is helpful or let them act as springboards to ideas and words which will help you 'come near to God' in your particular situation. Each day's outline includes:

Prayer
The prayer at the beginning picks up on one of the themes in the Bible verses. If thanks or prayer needs are mentioned, you might like to add specific things which are known to you and relevant to your particular situation. If helpful, encourage the person you are with to join in saying the 'Amen' at the end of the prayer.

Read
Try to use the same Bible every time you use these devotionals. If possible, choose one that the person with dementia is familiar with. It's hoped that the Bible and this booklet will be helpful cues for this time.

You might choose to use the whole Bible passage given or just the verse selection printed – whichever is easiest or most appropriate for your situation.

Talk about...

This section aims to start you thinking and talking about the Bible verses. It picks up words and ideas from the Bible passage to prompt thinking about the themes in ways which might help bring a sense of God's presence. Choose ideas that are appropriate and helpful in your situation.

Pray

You may like to say the Lord's Prayer each time you use one of these daily devotionals. It will probably have been familiar to many people and they may enjoy saying it aloud. It might be useful to use a traditional form of the prayer, for example:

Our Father, which art in heaven,
Hallowed be thy Name,
Thy kingdom come,
Thy will be done on earth as it is in heaven.
Give us this day our daily bread;
And forgive us our trespasses,
  as we forgive those who trespass against us;
And lead us not into temptation
  but deliver us from evil.
For thine is the kingdom, the power and
  the glory,
  forever and ever. Amen.

Hymn or song

You might like to sing together a favourite hymn of your own choice, or listen to the suggested track from the CD – created especially for this resource – included at the back of this volume.

The CD with its wide range of music – choral, brass band, children's choirs, a gospel group and soloists – has a hymn or song (or even a chorus from Sunday school days!) which links in with the theme of each day's Bible verses. You could sing along, or invite others to come and sing with you. However you choose to use it, we hope that these evocative recordings will bring God's comfort to those using this material.

Cues and clues box

The various suggestions are intended to act as cues and clues to the ideas and themes of the Bible verses. You might like to look at a picture, hold an object, listen to music or even paint in response to the day's devotional. Choose or adapt as most appropriate to the person with dementia, or older person, using this Bible and prayer guide.

DAILY BIBLE
READINGS

JESUS – WORDS...

...AND STORIES

GOD'S HEROES – FAITHFUL LIVES

Here are well-loved words of Jesus –
to bring us hope, comfort and a
confidence that God holds us in his
everlasting arms and welcomes us
into his presence.

THE BEATITUDES

CUES AND CLUES

Some of the following might help as you read today's verses from the Bible and pray.

Pictures
Photos of happy times; being held close by a parent.

Objects
A scarf or hot-water bottle (or something else to help you think about comfort).

To do
Extend a comforting gesture if appropriate (eg an arm around their shoulders).

PRAYER
Thank you, Father God, for your comfort and blessing. *Amen.*

READING Matthew 5:3–10

Blessed are the poor in spirit, for theirs is the kingdom of heaven. Blessed are those who mourn, for they will be comforted.
Matthew 5:3,4

TALK ABOUT...
☐ Not having much money
☐ Happy things and the good things in your life
☐ Examples of being comforted (eg someone you've seen crying)
☐ Times of being comforted (eg someone hugging you)
☐ God, like a parent, comforts us

PRAY
'Our Father, which art in heaven...'

HYMN OR SONG
'Praise God from whom all blessings flow'
(CD, *Words of faith*, track 1)

YOU ARE THE LIGHT
OF THE WORLD

CUES AND CLUES

Some of the following might help as you read today's verses from the Bible and pray.

Pictures
Photos of people doing good for others (eg parents; people serving others in some way; charity workers; nurses etc).

Objects
A torch or candle.

PRAYER

Lord Jesus, help us to share your light with others today. *Amen.*

READING Matthew 5:14–16

You are the light of the world. A city on a hill cannot be hidden. Neither do people light a lamp and put it under a bowl. Instead they put it on its stand, and it gives light to everyone in the house. In the same way, let your light shine before men, that they may see your good deeds and praise your Father in heaven.
Matthew 5:14–16

TALK ABOUT...

☐ Light, torches, candles
☐ Memories of being in the dark (eg at night, in wartime blackouts, in a cave)
☐ Good deeds – your own or others' for you
☐ Bringing God's light to others (eg a smile, good deeds you've done for others)
☐ Thankfulness to God for his light that we see in others

PRAY
'Our Father, which art in heaven…'

HYMN OR SONG
'Jesus wants me for a sunbeam'
(CD, *Words of faith*, track 2)

THE LORD'S PRAYER

PRAYER
Father God, thank you that you hear us when we pray, the prayers we say aloud and the unspoken prayers of our hearts. *Amen.*

READING Matthew 6:9–13

'Our Father in heaven, hallowed be your name, your kingdom come, your will be done on earth as it is in heaven. Give us today our daily bread. Forgive us our debts, as we also have forgiven our debtors. And lead us not into temptation, but deliver us from the evil one.'
Matthew 6:9–13

TALK ABOUT...
☐ Bread, other food
☐ Places you've heard the Lord's Prayer being said regularly (eg at school assembly, in church, in your family)
☐ What you pray about; how God has answered your prayers
☐ Thankfulness to God

PRAY
'Our Father, which art in heaven...'

HYMN OR SONG
'Father, hear the prayer we offer'
(CD, *Words of faith,* track 3)

DO NOT WORRY

CUES AND CLUES

Some of the following might help as you read today's verses from the Bible and pray.

Pictures
Birds; fashion pictures; barns full of hay or straw.

Objects
A cross to hold as you sing or listen to the song; fashion and consumer magazines.

To do
You could put some food on a bird table, hang up seeds or even go out and feed ducks on a local pond.

PRAYER
Lord God, we bring all our worries and anxieties to you now. Help us to leave them with you. *Amen.*

READING Matthew 6:25–27

Therefore I tell you, do not worry about your life, what you will eat or drink; or about your body, what you will wear. Is not life more important than food, and the body more important than clothes? Look at the birds of the air; they do not sow or reap or store away in barns, and yet your heavenly Father feeds them. Are you not much more valuable than they?
Matthew 6:25,26

TALK ABOUT…
☐ Birds (especially if this is a particular interest)
☐ Clothes, fashion
☐ What you worry about
☐ God gives us all we need
☐ Thankfulness to God

PRAY
'Our Father, which art in heaven…'

HYMN OR SONG
'All your anxiety'
(CD, *Words of faith*, track 4)

SEE HOW THE LILIES
OF THE FIELD GROW

CUES AND CLUES

Some of the following might help as you read today's verses from the Bible and pray.

Pictures
Flowers and gardens; beautiful scenes from nature.

Objects
Flowers, especially those you know are favourites – if possible with scent.

To do
Read these Bible verses and pray outside where you can see flowers; hold and smell sweet-scented flowers.

PRAYER
Father God, thank you for the beauty of your creation. Thank you for providing all that we need today. *Amen.*

READING Matthew 6:28–34

See how the lilies of the field grow. They do not labour or spin. Yet I tell you that not even Solomon in all his splendour was dressed like one of these. If that is how God clothes the grass of the field ... will he not much more clothe you ...? So do not worry ... But seek first his kingdom and his righteousness, and all these things will be given to you as well. *Matthew 6:28–31,33*

TALK ABOUT...
☐ Flowers; gardens; creation
☐ Today – what's happening now
☐ God being with us today
☐ Don't worry – God knows about all our needs

PRAY
'Our Father, which art in heaven...'

HYMN OR SONG
'All things bright and beautiful'
(CD, *Words of faith*, track 5)

ASK, SEEK, KNOCK

CUES AND CLUES

Some of the following might help as you read today's verses from the Bible and pray.

Pictures

The Light of theWorld by Holman Hunt; or *Praying Hands* by Albrecht Dürer.

Objects

A gift-wrapped present – with small gift that the person you are with will enjoy; a thimble; a door knocker or doorbell.

PRAYER

Father God, please hear our prayers today. Help us to discover your answers. *Amen.*

READING Matthew 7:7,8

Ask and it will be given to you; seek and you will find; knock and the door will be opened to you. For everyone who asks receives; he who seeks finds; and to him who knocks, the door will be opened.
Matthew 7:7,8

TALK ABOUT...

☐ Presents – receiving presents
☐ Asking and receiving
☐ Searching for things (eg the game of Hunt theThimble)
☐ Knocking on doors
☐ God hears when we ask, seek and knock
☐ Things you pray about – or want to pray about

PRAY

'Our Father, which art in heaven…'

HYMN OR SONG

'Kum ba yah my Lord'
(CD, *Words of faith*, track 6)

THE HOUSE
ON THE ROCK

CUES AND CLUES

Some of the following might help as you read today's verses from the Bible and pray.

Pictures
Seaside, sandcastles, rocks, foundations, tall buildings.

Objects
Sand, beach pebbles; the Bible (ie God's Word).

PRAYER
Lord Jesus, thank you that we can trust your words. Help us to hear and build our lives on them. *Amen.*

READING Matthew 7:24–27

Therefore everyone who hears these words of mine and puts them into practice is like a wise man who built his house on the rock. The rain came down, the streams rose, and the winds blew and beat against that house; yet it did not fall, because it had its foundation on the rock. *Matthew 7:24,25*

TALK ABOUT...
☐ Sandcastles – what happens when the sea comes in
☐ Rocks, foundations, building
☐ We can rely on Jesus' words in the Bible

PRAY
'Our Father, which art in heaven...'

HYMN OR SONG
'The wise man built his house upon the rock' (CD, *Words of faith*, track 7)

REST FOR
THE WEARY

PRAYER
Lord Jesus, help us not to be worried or troubled. Thank you that we can find rest in you. *Amen.*

READING Matthew 11:28–30

Come to me, all you who are weary and burdened, and I will give you rest. Take my yoke upon you and learn from me, for I am gentle and humble in heart, and you will find rest for your souls. For my yoke is easy and my burden is light.
Matthew 11:28–30

TALK ABOUT...
☐ Carrying heavy burdens (eg shopping, books)
☐ Rest – a favourite armchair, lying on a beach, going to sleep at night in bed
☐ Feeling burdened with troubles – Jesus wants to help us carry them

PRAY
'Our Father, which art in heaven...'

HYMN OR SONG
'For all the saints'
(CD, *Words of faith*, track 8)

I AM
WITH YOU

CUES AND CLUES

Some of the following might help as you read today's verses from the Bible and pray.

Pictures
Baptism (might be a photo); two friends walking together; footprints in the sand (you might also like to read the poem 'Footprints in the sand', anon).

Objects
Sandals or shoes; some water; a cross.

PRAYER
Lord Jesus, help me to follow you. Thank you that you are always with me. *Amen.*

READING Matthew 28:19,20

Therefore go and make disciples of all nations, baptising them in the name of the Father and of the Son and of the Holy Spirit, and teaching them to obey everything I have commanded you. And surely I am with you always, to the very end of the age.
Matthew 28:19,20

TALK ABOUT...
☐ Being a 'disciple' of Jesus
☐ Your own story of following Jesus
☐ Jesus' promise to be with us – always

PRAY
'Our Father, which art in heaven...'

HYMN OR SONG
'God be with you till we meet again'
(CD, *Words of faith*, track 9)

I AM THE
BREAD OF LIFE

CUES AND CLUES

Some of the following might help as you read today's verses from the Bible and pray.

Pictures
Bread, waterfalls; Jesus at the Last Supper or the feeding of the 5,000 (eg fine art or picture in a Bible storybook).

Objects
A loaf of bread; cold water.

To do
Share a fresh bread roll; drink some water.

PRAYER
Lord Jesus, help us to come to you today. Thank you that you know all my needs. *Amen.*

READING John 6:35

I am the bread of life. He who comes to me will never go hungry, and he who believes in me will never be thirsty.
John 6:35

TALK ABOUT...
☐ Bread; favourite drinks
☐ Food and drink when you're hungry or thirsty (eg a cold drink on a hot summer's day)
☐ What's for lunch or supper today
☐ Jesus promises that if we come to him he will meet all our needs

PRAY
'Our Father, which art in heaven…'

HYMN OR SONG
'Guide me, O thou great Jehovah'
(CD, *Words of faith*, track 10)

I AM THE
GOOD SHEPHERD

CUES AND CLUES

Some of the following might help as you read today's verses from the Bible and pray.

Pictures

Sheep and shepherds; a fine art picture of Jesus on the cross.

Objects

Sheepskin (eg rug, slippers); a 'toy' sheep to hold; a simple cross.

PRAYER

Lord Jesus, thank you that you are my Good Shepherd and you care for me. Help me to stay close to you today. *Amen.*

READING John 10:14,15

I am the good shepherd; I know my sheep and my sheep know me – just as the Father knows me and I know the Father – and I lay down my life for the sheep.
John 10:14,15

TALK ABOUT…

☐ Sheep; shepherds

☐ How Jesus is like a shepherd to us

☐ Jesus loves us and gave his life for us

PRAY

'Our Father, which art in heaven…'

HYMN OR SONG

'The King of love my shepherd is'
(CD, *Words of faith*, track 11)

12

DO NOT LET YOUR
HEARTS BE TROUBLED

CUES AND CLUES

Some of the following might help as you read today's verses from the Bible and pray.

Pictures
Rooms – might be photos of your own house or room.

Objects
A doll's house.

PRAYER
Lord Jesus, we bring our troubles to you. You know what is on our hearts and minds. Help us to trust in you now. *Amen.*

READING John 14:1–4

Do not let your hearts be troubled. Trust in God; trust also in me. In my Father's house are many rooms; if it were not so, I would have told you. I am going there to prepare a place for you. And if I go and prepare a place for you, I will come back and take you to be with me that you also may be where I am.
John 14:1–3

TALK ABOUT...
☐ Your bedroom; your home
☐ Worries
☐ What Jesus says to us (eg 'Don't worry about...')
☐ Jesus is with us now – and always will be

PRAY
'Our Father, which art in heaven...'

HYMN OR SONG
'When all thy mercies, O my God'
(CD, *Words of faith*, track 12)

MY PEACE
I GIVE YOU

CUES AND CLUES

Some of the following might help as you read today's verses from the Bible and pray.

Pictures
Photos of a peaceful sunset, garden, river or sea; a dove.

Objects
Some simple white flowers.

To do
Spend a few moments in silence, listening to the quiet; read today's Bible verses and prayers in a garden.

PRAYER
Lord Jesus, thank you for your peace with us here. Whatever our fears, frustrations or worries we bring them to you now. Help us to receive your peace today. *Amen.*

READING John 14:25–27

**Peace I leave with you; my peace I give you.
I do not give to you as the world gives.
Do not let your hearts be troubled and do
not be afraid.**
John 14:27

TALK ABOUT...
☐ Peace and quietness
☐ Being afraid; frustrations and worries
☐ Accepting the peace which Jesus offers to us today

PRAY
'Our Father, which art in heaven...'

HYMN OR SONG
'New every morning is the love'
(CD, *Words of faith*, track 13)

Listen again to these 'stories of Jesus'.
As you do so, may you hear his voice
and be aware of his compassion and
care for you.

THE SOWER

Some of the following might help as you read today's verses from the Bible and pray.

Pictures
A harvest field; *The Sower* by Van Gogh.

Objects
Seeds; some wheat; a seedling in a pot.

PRAYER
Lord God, may your good seed grow in me and bring your life and love to others. *Amen.*

READING Luke 8:4–8

A farmer went out to sow his seed. As he was scattering the seed, some fell along the path; it was trampled on, and the birds of the air ate it up. Some fell on rock ... Other seed fell among thorns ... Still other seed fell on good soil. It came up and yielded a crop, a hundred times more than was sown.
Luke 8:5–8

TALK ABOUT...
☐ Farmers sowing their crops
☐ Harvest time
☐ Gardening; growing plants
☐ The good things God wants to see growing in our lives

PRAY
'Our Father, which art in heaven...'

HYMN OR SONG
'For the beauty of the earth'
(CD, *Words of faith,* track 14)

THE MUSTARD SEED

CUES AND CLUES

Some of the following might help as you read today's verses from the Bible and pray.

Pictures
A very large tree; a bird's nest in a tree; children climbing trees; your church.

Objects
Seeds; a branch; an old bird's nest.

PRAYER
Lord God, thank you for the shelter we find in you. *Amen.*

READING Mark 4:30–32

Again he said, 'What shall we say the kingdom of God is like, or what parable shall we use to describe it? It is like a mustard seed, which is the smallest seed you plant in the ground. Yet when planted, it grows and becomes the largest of all garden plants, with such big branches that the birds of the air can perch in its shade.'
Mark 4:30–32

TALK ABOUT...
☐ Seeds, gardening, big plants, trees
☐ Birds and bird-watching
☐ Trees and their shade;
   tree houses of childhood
☐ The shelter God offers;
   the worldwide Church

PRAY
'Our Father, which art in heaven...'

HYMN OR SONG
'He's got the whole world in his hands'
(CD, *Words of faith*, track 15)

HIDDEN TREASURE

CUES AND CLUES

Some of the following might help as you read today's verses from the Bible and pray.

Pictures
Treasure; a pearl necklace; Jesus on the cross.

Objects
A jewellery box; a pearl necklace; a cross.

PRAYER
Lord God, thank you that you love us so much you gave your Son Jesus for us. *Amen.*

READING Matthew 13:44–46

The kingdom of heaven is like treasure hidden in a field. When a man found it, he hid it again, and then in his joy went and sold all he had and bought that field.
Matthew 13:44

TALK ABOUT...
☐ Treasure; precious things; treasure hunts; pearls or jewellery
☐ God's love for us is more valuable than anything
☐ We are very special and valuable to God
☐ In Jesus, God gives everything for us

PRAY
'Our Father, which art in heaven…'

HYMN OR SONG
'There is a green hill far away'
(CD, *Words of faith*, track 16)

THE GOOD SAMARITAN

PRAYER
Lord God, help us today to show care for those around us. *Amen.*

READING Luke 10:30–37

A man was going down from Jerusalem to Jericho, when he fell into the hands of robbers. They stripped him of his clothes, beat him and went away, leaving him half-dead. A priest happened to be going down the same road, and ... passed by .... So too, a Levite passed by ... But a Samaritan, as he travelled ... when he saw him, he took pity on him.
Luke 10:30–33

TALK ABOUT...
☐ Neighbours
☐ God wants us to share his love with our neighbours – those around us
☐ Ways in which we are doing that

PRAY
'Our Father, which art in heaven...'

HYMN OR SONG
'O brother man, fold to thy heart thy brother'
(CD, *Words of faith*, track 17)

29

THE LOST SHEEP

Some of the following might help as you read today's verses from the Bible and pray.

Pictures
Shepherd and sheep; Jesus as the Good Shepherd.

Objects
A sheepskin rug or something else made of sheepskin (eg slippers, hat, gloves); a 'toy' sheep to hold (even a glove puppet!); a shepherd's crook.

PRAYER
Lord God, thank you that you love us so much you gave your Son Jesus for us. Help us when we're lost, and bring us close to you. *Amen.*

READING Luke 15:3–7

Suppose one of you has a hundred sheep and loses one of them. Does he not leave the ninety-nine in the open country and go after the lost sheep until he finds it?
Luke 15:4

TALK ABOUT...
☐ Sheep, lambs; playing hide-and-seek; losing things that are special to us
☐ God's love for us – we are very special and valuable to God
☐ Jesus, the Good Shepherd, keeps us safe

PRAY
'Our Father, which art in heaven…'

HYMN OR SONG
'Saviour, like a shepherd lead us'
(CD, *Words of faith*, track 18)

THE LOST COIN

CUES AND CLUES

Some of the following might help as you read today's verses from the Bible and pray.

Pictures
Lost property sign.

Objects
Coins; a lost property box.

PRAYER
Lord God, when we feel we are lost, help us to know that we are safe with you. *Amen.*

READING Luke 15:8–10

Or suppose a woman has ten silver coins and loses one. Does she not light a lamp, sweep the house and search carefully until she finds it? And when she finds it, she calls her friends and neighbours together and says, 'Rejoice with me; I have found my lost coin.'
Luke 15:8,9

TALK ABOUT...
☐ House cleaning; losing and finding special things (eg money, keys, photos)
☐ God searches for us – we are safe with him
☐ God loves us – we are very special and valuable to him

PRAY
'Our Father, which art in heaven...'

HYMN OR SONG
'I will sing the wondrous story'
(CD, *Words of faith,* track 19)

THE PRODIGAL SON

CUES AND CLUES

Some of the following might help as you read today's verses from the Bible and pray.

Pictures
A 'Welcome home' sign; *The Return of the Prodigal Son* by Rembrandt.

Objects
'Welcome home' sign; streamers etc to suggest celebration.

PRAYER
Heavenly Father, help us to come to you now. Thank you that you welcome us and accept us as we are. *Amen.*

READING Luke 15:11–24

But while he was still a long way off, his father saw him and was filled with compassion for him; he ran to his son, threw his arms around him and kissed him.
Luke 15:20

TALK ABOUT...
☐ Adventures of teenagers or young adults; our own teenage escapades
☐ God loves us like a parent
☐ Even when we make mistakes or have gone away from him, he keeps on loving us
☐ God welcomes us when we come to him

PRAY
'Our Father, which art in heaven…'

HYMN OR SONG
'Come, let us sing of a wonderful love'
(CD, *Words of faith*, track 20)

GOD'S HEROES –
FAITHFUL LIVES

These well-loved stories of God's heroes encourage us to stand firm in our faith and to keep trusting in his faithfulness to us.

NOAH AND
THE ARK

PRAYER
Lord God, thank you that you provide for us and
keep us safe in troubled times. *Amen.*

READING Genesis 6:9–22

**Noah was a righteous man, blameless ... and
he walked with God. ... Now the earth was
corrupt in God's sight and was full of violence.
... God said to Noah, '... make yourself an
ark of cypress wood ... I am going to bring
floodwaters on the earth ... But I will establish
my covenant with you, and you will enter the
ark ... You are to bring into the ark two of all
living creatures ...' Noah did everything just
as God commanded him.**
Genesis 6:9,11,13,14,17–19,22

TALK ABOUT...
☐ The story of Noah and the ark; reminiscences
  of where you first heard this story
☐ Rain and floods
☐ Animals
☐ God keeps us safe in stormy times

PRAY
'Our Father, which art in heaven...'

HYMN OR SONG
'Mr Noah built an ark'
(CD, *Words of faith*, track 21)

22

NOAH AND
THE RAINBOW

CUES AND CLUES

Some of the following might help as you read today's verses from the Bible and pray.

Pictures
Rainbows; photos of rainbows.

Objects
Ribbons in the colours of the rainbow.

To do
If you enjoy painting, paint a rainbow.

PRAYER
Lord God, thank you for the rainbow which reminds us of your faithfulness to us. *Amen.*

READING Genesis 8:1,15–19; 9:1,14–16

Then God said to Noah, 'Come out of the ark ... Bring every kind of living creature that is with you ... be fruitful and increase in number ... I have set my rainbow in the clouds ...Whenever the rainbow appears ... I will see it and remember the everlasting covenant between God and all living creatures of every kind on the earth.'
Genesis 8:15,17; 9:13,16

TALK ABOUT...
☐ The story of Noah and the ark
☐ Rainbows
☐ God promises to be faithful to his people

PRAY
'Our Father, which art in heaven...'

HYMN OR SONG
'Great is thy faithfulness'
(CD, *Words of faith*, track 22)

THE CALL OF ABRAM

CUES AND CLUES

Some of the following might help as you read today's verses from the Bible and pray.

Pictures
Desert landscape with nomads; travel scenes or camping.

Objects
A map or guidebook; a compass.

PRAYER
Lord God, guide us and keep us. Help us to hear you and obey your Word. *Amen.*

READING Genesis 12:1–9

The LORD had said to Abram, 'Leave your country, your people and your father's household and go to the land I will show you. I will make you into a great nation and I will bless you … and all peoples on earth will be blessed through you.' So Abram left, as the LORD had told him …
Genesis 12:1–4

TALK ABOUT…
☐ Setting out on a long journey
☐ Examples you know of how God has led individuals
☐ God guides us

PRAY
'Our Father, which art in heaven…'

HYMN OR SONG
'Thy hand, O God, has guided'
(CD, *Words of faith*, track 23)

JOSEPH AND
HIS DREAMS

PRAYER
Lord God, thank you for the ways in which you
are at work in our lives today. *Amen.*

READING Genesis 37:1–11

**Now Israel loved Joseph more than any
of his other sons ... and he made a richly
ornamented robe for him. ... Joseph had a
dream ... 'Listen ... the sun and moon and
eleven stars were bowing down to me.' ... His
brothers were jealous of him, but his father
kept the matter in mind.**
Genesis 37:3,5,9,11

TALK ABOUT...
- ☐ Dreams
- ☐ Special clothes (a dress, a uniform)
- ☐ Brothers and sisters – our relationships
  with them as children or adults
- ☐ God was working in Joseph's life
  from his youth
- ☐ Special times when God has worked in your life

PRAY
'Our Father, which art in heaven...'

HYMN OR SONG
'Heaven came down and glory filled my soul'
(CD, *Words of faith*, track 24)

MOSES IN THE BULRUSHES

<table>
<tr><td>

CUES AND CLUES

Some of the following might help as you read today's verses from the Bible and pray.

Pictures
Reeds near a river; a baby in a cradle.

Objects
A Moses basket; a crib or cradle; bulrushes.

</td></tr>
</table>

PRAYER
Lord God, thank you for the ways in which you protect us and work out your purposes for us and others throughout our lives. *Amen.*

READING Exodus 2:1–10

Now a man of the house of Levi married a Levite woman, and she became pregnant and gave birth to a son. … when she could hide him no longer, she got a papyrus basket for him and coated it with tar and pitch. Then she placed the child in it and put it among the reeds along the bank of the Nile.
Exodus 2:1–3

TALK ABOUT...
☐ Babies; cradles and cribs
☐ The story of Moses in the bulrushes
☐ God was working out his plans in Moses' life from babyhood – and keeping him safe
☐ God is at work in our lives

PRAY
'Our Father, which art in heaven…'

HYMN OR SONG
'God is working his purpose out'
(CD, *Words of faith,* track 25)

MOSES AND THE BURNING BUSH

CUES AND CLUES

Some of the following might help as you read today's verses from the Bible and pray.

Pictures
A bush; sandals.

Objects
Sandals; a burning candle.

To do
If you are comfortable doing so, remove your shoes as you think about being in God's presence.

PRAYER
Holy Lord, thank you for speaking to us and calling us to serve you. *Amen.*

READING Exodus 3:1–12

There the angel of the LORD appeared to him in flames of fire from within a bush. Moses saw that though the bush was on fire it did not burn up. … God called to him from within the bush, 'Moses! Moses! … Take off your sandals, for the place where you are standing is holy ground. … I am sending you to Pharaoh to bring my people the Israelites out of Egypt.'
Exodus 3:2,4,5,10

TALK ABOUT…
- ☐ The story of Moses and the burning bush
- ☐ God is holy
- ☐ God promises to be with Moses to help him
- ☐ What we have been called to do in our lives
- ☐ God is with us

PRAY
'Our Father, which art in heaven…'

HYMN OR SONG
'Holy, holy, holy'
(CD, *Words of faith*, track 26)

MOSES AND THE RED SEA

CUES AND CLUES

Some of the following might help as you read today's verses from the Bible and pray.

Pictures
Looking at the sea from a beach.

Objects
Dry sand.

PRAYER

Almighty God, help us to trust you. Please guide us and protect us when we are uncertain. *Amen.*

READING Exodus 14:10,13,21,22,26–31

Moses answered ... 'Do not be afraid. Stand firm and you will see the deliverance the LORD will bring you today. ... Then Moses stretched out his hand over the sea ... The waters were divided, and the Israelites went through the sea on dry ground ...
Exodus 14:13,21,22

TALK ABOUT...
☐ Feeling afraid; times when you've been in a frightening situation and how you were rescued
☐ The story of the Israelites crossing the Red Sea
☐ God looks after his people – we can rely on him

PRAY
'Our Father, which art in heaven...'

HYMN OR SONG
'How did Moses cross the Red Sea?'
(CD, *Words of faith*, track 27)

THE CALL
OF SAMUEL

PRAYER

Lord God, thank you that you know us by name. Help us to listen to you today. *Amen.*

READING 1 Samuel 3:1–10

The Lord called Samuel a third time, and Samuel got up and went to Eli and said, 'Here I am; you called me.' Then Eli realised that the Lord was calling the boy. ... So Samuel went and lay down in his place. The Lord came and stood there, calling as at the other times, 'Samuel! Samuel!' Then Samuel said, 'Speak, for your servant is listening.'
1 Samuel 3:8–10

TALK ABOUT...

☐ Where you sleep; your bedroom as a child
☐ Calling out to catch someone's attention
   (times when this has happened today)
☐ Samuel's story
☐ God speaks to us and knows us by name

PRAY

'Our Father, which art in heaven...'

HYMN OR SONG

'Master, speak! Thy servant heareth'
(CD, *Words of faith*, track 28)

DAVID AND GOLIATH

PRAYER

Lord Almighty, help us with all the challenges that face us today. Thank you that you give us your strength. *Amen.*

READING 1 Samuel 17:34–40,45–50

Then he ... chose five smooth stones from the stream, put them in the pouch of his shepherd's bag, and with his sling in his hand, approached the Philistine. ... David said ... 'You come against me with sword and spear ... but I come against you in the name of the LORD Almighty ...' ... Reaching into his bag and taking out a stone, he slung it and struck the Philistine on the forehead. ... and he fell face down on the ground.
1 Samuel 17:40,45,49

TALK ABOUT...

☐ Fights; catapults; stones from a stream
☐ The story of David and Goliath
☐ God gives us strength even though we are weak

PRAY
'Our Father, which art in heaven...'

HYMN OR SONG
'Only a boy called David'
(CD, *Words of faith*, track 29)

SHADRACH, MESHACH AND ABEDNEGO

CUES AND CLUES

Some of the following might help as you read today's verses from the Bible and pray.

Pictures
Fires; a baking oven.

Objects
Kindling wood, newspapers scrunched up as if to make a fire, a coal scuttle with coal; a cross – or other symbol of God's presence with you.

PRAYER
Lord Jesus, thank you that you walk with us through difficult times. Help us to know that you are with us now. *Amen.*

READING Daniel 3:13–28

Then King Nebuchadnezzar leaped to his feet in amazement ... 'Weren't there three men that we tied up and threw into the fire? ... Look! I see four men walking around in the fire, unbound and unharmed, and the fourth looks like a son of the gods.'
Daniel 3:24,25

TALK ABOUT...
☐ Bonfires; fires used for smelting; bakers' ovens
☐ Burns you've suffered
☐ The story of Shadrach, Meshach and Abednego in the fiery furnace
☐ God, or his angels, being with you in difficult situations

PRAY
'Our Father, which art in heaven...'

HYMN OR SONG
'Praise to the Lord, the Almighty'
(CD, *Words of faith*, track 30)

DANIEL IN
THE LIONS' DEN

CUES AND CLUES

Some of the following might help as you read today's verses from the Bible and pray.

Pictures
Lions; angels.

Objects
A small pet cage; a Christmas tree 'angel'; a cross – or other symbol of God's presence with you.

PRAYER

Lord God, thank you that you promise to protect us in difficult times. Please keep us safe today. *Amen.*

READING Daniel 6:10–16,19–23

So the king gave the order, and they brought Daniel and threw him into the lions' den. … At the first light of dawn, the king got up and hurried to the lions' den. … 'Daniel, servant of the living God, has your God, whom you serve continually, been able to rescue you from the lions?' Daniel answered, 'O king, live for ever! My God sent his angel, and he shut the mouths of the lions.'
Daniel 6:16,19–22

TALK ABOUT…
☐ Lions
☐ Frightening times
☐ The story of Daniel in the lions' den
☐ God is with us, whatever our situation

PRAY
'Our Father, which art in heaven…'

HYMN OR SONG
'Dare to be a Daniel'
(CD, *Words of faith*, track 31)

FURTHER
RESOURCES

Worship with people with dementia

'Holy, Holy, Holy': The church's ministry with people with dementia by Jackie Treetops, available from Faith in Elderly People (contact details, page 46).

The Wells of Life: Moments of worship with people with dementia by Gaynor Hammond and Jackie Treetops, available from Faith in Elderly People (contact details, page 46).

Worship for People with Dementia, a booklet based on material by Margaret Goodall, Gaynor Hammond and Laraine Moffitt, available from MHA (contact details, page 46).

Hymns and songs

There are several good websites where you can find words and music for hymns and songs. Try: www.cyberhymnal.org

Memory and reminiscence

Memories are Made of This: Reminiscence activities for person-centred care by Julie Heathcote, available from Alzheimer's Society (contact details, page 46).

The Memory Box by Gaynor Hammond, available from Faith in Elderly People (contact details, page 46).

Pictures to Share These books of pictures are ideal for sharing with people with dementia. Themes covered in the titles include: Childhood, Funny Old World, In the Garden, Beside the Seaside, A Sporting Life, The Countryside, A Woman's Work, Travelling, Shopping, Pets. Available from: www.picturestoshare.co.uk

For carers and churches

In a Strange Land: People with dementia and the church by Malcolm Goldsmith, available from 4M Publications: www.4mpublications.co.uk; or: www.amazon.co.uk

USEFUL
CONTACT DETAILS

MHA
Epworth House,
Stuart Street,
Derby DE1 2EQ

01332 296200
enquiries@mha.org.uk
www.mha.org.uk

**Christian Council
on Ageing**
info@ccoa.org.uk
www.ccoa.org.uk

Faith in Elderly People
Publications:
Gaynor Hammond
29 Silverdale Avenue,
Guiseley,
Leeds, LS20 8BD

01943 879320
gaynor.hammond@northern.org.uk

Alzheimer's Society
Devon House,
58 St Katharine's Way,
London E1W 1JX

+44 (0) 20 7423 3500
enquiries@alzheimers.org.uk
www.alzheimers.org.uk

BEING WITH GOD

A Bible and prayer guide
for people with dementia

OTHER TITLES AVAILABLE
IN THIS SERIES:

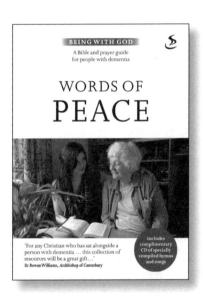

Words of hope

- Jesus – light and life
- Psalms – words of hope

ISBN 9781844275205

Words of peace

- In the beginning, God…
- Peace – through Jesus

ISBN: 9781844275229

£6.99 each

Available from your local **Christian bookshop**
from **www.scriptureunion.org.uk/shop**
or from Scripture Union Mail Order on **0845 07 06 006**

CD:
WORDS OF FAITH

Hymns and songs

1 'Praise God from whom all
blessings flow'
2 'Jesus wants me for a sunbeam'
3 'Father, hear the prayer we offer'
4 'All your anxiety'
5 'All things bright and beautiful'
6 'Kum ba yah my Lord'
7 'The wise man built his house
upon the rock'
8 'For all the saints'
9 'God be with you till we meet again'
10 'Guide me, O thou great Jehovah'
11 'The King of love my shepherd is'
12 'When all thy mercies, O my God'
13 'New every morning is the love'
14 'For the beauty of the earth'
15 'He's got the whole world in his hands'
16 'There is a green hill far away'
17 'O brother man, fold to thy heart
thy brother'
18 'Saviour, like a shepherd lead us'
19 'I will sing the wondrous story'
20 'Come, let us sing of a wonderful love'
21 'Mr Noah built an ark'
22 'Great is thy faithfulness'
23 'Thy hand, O God, has guided'
24 'Heaven came down and glory
filled my soul'

25 'God is working his purpose out'
26 'Holy, holy, holy'
27 'How did Moses cross the Red Sea?'
28 'Master, speak! Thy servant heareth'
29 'Only a boy called David'
30 'Praise to the Lord, the Almighty'
31 'Dare to be a Daniel'

Acknowledgements:
Original recordings made at Frog Studios, Cheshire
and on location by **Gordon Lorenz**.

Featuring...
Vocalists: Ian Wallace, Jean Barrowman, Valerie Monese,
Hero Douglas, John Delbridge.
Choirs: St George's Chapel Choir, Windsor Castle;
Treorchy Male Voice Choir; The Choir of Guildford
Cathedral; The Massed Choirs of Yorkshire; The
Castleford Singers; The Gordon Lorenz Singers;
Colwyn Bay Children's Choir.
Musicians: The Brighouse and Rastrick Brass Band,
Matthew Freeman, Steve Millington, Barry Thompson.

Engineers: Mark Walker and Richard Scott.

Mastered at RAS Studios, Manchester. All recordings
produced by **Gordon Lorenz**.